ARCHER CURTIS

Beyond the Past

Mastering the Art of Letting Go and Moving Forward

Contents

1

Chapter 1: The Burden of Holding On

Why We Struggle to Let Go

Holding onto the past—whether it's a failed relationship, a missed opportunity, or a painful memory—can feel like carrying a heavy burden. We cling to it, believing that by holding on, we can somehow make sense of what happened, or worse, change it. But the reality is that holding on only drags us down, limiting our ability to grow and thrive.

Imagine walking through life with a heavy backpack filled with regrets, anger, and unfulfilled expectations. Over time, the weight becomes unbearable. You might not notice it at first, but the tension, stress, and constant reminders eventually wear you down. This is the emotional and psychological toll of holding on.

Anna and the Weight of Resentment

Anna, a 35-year-old marketing executive, had been carrying the burden of resentment for over a decade. In her early twenties, she was deeply in love with her college boyfriend, Jason. They had made big plans for the future, but one day, without warning, Jason left her for another woman. The betrayal left Anna shattered. Even years after the breakup, she couldn't shake the feeling of anger and rejection.

Despite being successful in her career, Anna's personal life remained stagnant. Every time she tried to build a new relationship, the memories of Jason would resurface, reminding her of the pain. Her resentment became a filter through which she viewed all her relationships—distrustful, guarded, and always waiting for the other shoe to drop. It wasn't until Anna realized that her inability to let go of the past was preventing her from moving forward that she decided to make a change. But the process was slow and painful, as it often is.

Why Do We Hold On?

The reasons we hold on to the past are complex and varied, often tied to our emotions, psychology, and need for control. Here are some common reasons:

1) Fear of the Unknown

Letting go means stepping into uncertainty. We may not like where we are, but at least it's familiar. The thought of venturing into the unknown without the baggage of our past feels risky and frightening. People often think, "If I let go, what will replace it?"

2) Emotional Investment

We invest emotionally in people, situations, and outcomes. The more we invest, the harder it becomes to let go. It's not just about losing a person or opportunity, but the emotional time and energy that went into it. Letting go feels like admitting that the investment didn't pay off.

3) Unresolved Emotions

Many people cling to the past because of unresolved feelings—anger, guilt, sadness. These emotions act like hooks, keeping us tethered to the past. Until we face them head-on, they'll continue to hold us back.

4) The Illusion of Control

There's a sense of control in holding on. We believe that if we keep replaying the past, analyzing every detail, and staying angry, we can somehow change what happened. This is an illusion. The past is unchangeable, and holding on only keeps us stuck.

Research Insight: The Psychological Toll of Holding On

Research from the field of psychology backs up the idea that holding onto past emotional pain negatively impacts mental health. According to a study published in the *Journal of Behavioral Therapy*, people who habitually revisit past hurts are more likely to suffer from depression and anxiety. The constant replaying of negative events creates a loop, reinforcing feelings of powerlessness and hopelessness.

Neuroscientists have also found that holding onto emotional pain can increase cortisol levels, the stress hormone. Chronic stress from unresolved emotions leads to a host of physical issues, including insomnia, headaches, and even heart disease.

Breaking the Chains: Recognizing the Signs You're Holding On

The first step in letting go is recognizing when you're holding on to something that no longer serves you. Here are some common signs:

1) Constantly Replaying the Past

If you find yourself frequently thinking about a past event or conversation, trying to figure out where it went wrong, that's a sign you're holding on.

2) Feeling Stuck or Stagnant

Emotional baggage often manifests as a feeling of being stuck in life—whether it's in relationships, career, or personal growth.

3) Unresolved Anger or Resentment

Holding grudges or resentment towards others, even years after the incident, is a clear indication that you haven't let go.

4) Difficulty Moving On

Whether it's in relationships or new opportunities, if you find yourself unable to fully embrace the present because of past memories, you're still holding on.

Here's an interesting Case Study:

The Company That Couldn't Move Forward

A notable case in the business world is that of Blockbuster, the once-dominant video rental company. At its peak, Blockbuster could have acquired Netflix for a fraction of its current value. However, the company was deeply attached to its traditional model of physical rentals and resisted embracing the new, digital streaming trend. Blockbuster held on to its past success, believing it would continue, despite clear signs that the industry was shifting. Ultimately, their refusal to let go of their old business model led to their downfall. Netflix, meanwhile, thrived by constantly adapting and letting go of outdated strategies.

This case illustrates how holding onto the past, whether in personal or professional life, can prevent growth and lead to stagnation or failure.

Exercise: The Emotional Backpack

To help you recognize the emotional weight you're carrying, imagine your emotions and unresolved issues as items in a backpack.

- **Step 1**: Write down everything that weighs you down—regrets, past relationships, fears, anger, guilt, etc. Each one is an item that you place in the backpack.
- **Step 2**: Visualize how heavy this backpack becomes as you

add more items. Feel the weight.

- **Step 3**: Now, imagine yourself slowly taking out one item at a time. How does the backpack feel as it becomes lighter?
- **Step 4**: Write down how your life might improve if you could lighten your emotional load. What could you do without that weight?

This simple visualization exercise helps make the emotional weight we carry more tangible, encouraging the process of letting go.

Understanding the Impact of Holding On

By the end of this chapter, readers should understand that holding on to the past doesn't protect them; it hinders them. It is a burden that weighs us down emotionally, mentally, and even physically. To move forward, we must first be willing to recognize the ways in which we're holding on, and then take steps toward releasing that weight.

2

Chapter 2: The Psychology Behind Letting Go

Why Letting Go Feels Like a Battle

Letting go often feels like a battle against our own instincts. Our brains are wired to seek stability and comfort, which means that stepping away from familiar but unhealthy situations can feel like walking into the unknown. This chapter explores the psychological mechanisms that make letting go a struggle, including our attachment systems, the fear of uncertainty, and cognitive dissonance.

Mark's Struggle to Move On

Mark's experience with his business partner highlights a common struggle with letting go. After his partner left, Mark became fixated on what went wrong. He reviewed every interaction, tried to analyze the betrayal from every angle, and even imagined confrontations. Mark's attachment to the past and need to make sense of it prevented him from moving forward.

Over time, Mark's obsession with the betrayal began to affect his health and well-being. He experienced insomnia, anxiety, and a loss of motivation in his work. The emotional weight of holding onto the past started to manifest physically, impacting his relationships and productivity. It was only through therapy and self-reflection that Mark began to understand how his need for control and understanding was keeping him stuck. By confronting his fear of uncertainty and focusing on his present and future, he slowly began to release the grip of his past pain.

The Science of Attachment: Why Our Minds Resist Letting Go

Understanding the brain's role in attachment and resistance to change can shed light on why letting go is so difficult. Our brains are designed to form and maintain attachments to people, ideas, and routines. This attachment system is crucial for survival, but it can also trap us in cycles of attachment that hinder our growth.

1. **Fear of Uncertainty**
2. The brain's aversion to uncertainty is deeply rooted in our evolutionary history. Early humans needed predictability for survival—knowing where their next meal was coming from or avoiding danger. In modern times, this instinct manifests as a fear of change. When faced with uncertainty, our brain's amygdala, the emotional center, triggers a stress response, making us cling to what's familiar even if it's no longer beneficial.

- **Research Insight**: A study published in *Neuropsychology* highlights that uncertainty activates the brain's threat detection system. This leads to increased anxiety and a preference for familiar, even if distressing, situations.

2.Loss Aversion

Loss aversion, a concept from behavioral economics, explains why we fear letting go. According to Daniel Kahneman and Amos Tversky's research, the pain of losing something is psychologically about twice as powerful as the pleasure of gaining something. This means that the potential loss from letting go feels more threatening than the potential benefits of embracing something new.

- **Case Study**: In one study, participants were given a choice between a sure gain of $100 or a 50% chance to win $250. Most chose the sure gain, despite the fact that the expected value was higher with the gamble. This illustrates how loss aversion influences decision-making.

3.Cognitive Dissonance

Cognitive dissonance arises when we hold conflicting beliefs or attitudes, creating mental discomfort. For example, if we believe we should be happy but are stuck in an unhappy relationship, the dissonance between these beliefs can be overwhelming. To alleviate this discomfort, we might rationalize staying in the relationship or avoid confronting the underlying issues.

- **Research Insight**: A study in *Social Psychological and Personality Science* found that people often change their attitudes to align with their behaviors to reduce cognitive dissonance.

This can lead to maintaining unhealthy patterns rather than facing the discomfort of change.

Case Study:

The Business Leader Who Couldn't Let Go

Kodak's story provides a powerful example of how attachment to past success can prevent adaptation and growth. Kodak, once a leader in film photography, failed to embrace the digital revolution. Despite having the technology and opportunity to pivot, Kodak's management clung to their traditional film business, believing that it would continue to dominate the market.

The company's attachment to its legacy was a major factor in its downfall. Kodak's inability to let go of its past success and adapt to new market trends led to its bankruptcy. This case underscores the dangers of attachment and the importance of embracing change to ensure long-term success.

- **Additional Insight**: The rise of digital photography was driven by changing consumer preferences and technological advancements. Kodak's resistance to these changes is a classic example of how clinging to outdated models can lead to failure.

Why We Become Emotionally Attached
Emotional attachment is a fundamental aspect of human

experience. We form attachments to people, ideas, and routines, which provide us with a sense of security and identity. Understanding why these attachments are so strong can help us navigate the process of letting go.

1.Emotional Investment

The sunk cost fallacy explains why we struggle to let go of things we've invested heavily in. When we invest significant emotional, financial, or time resources into something, we become attached to it. Letting go feels like admitting that the investment was a waste, which is a painful realization.

- Consider a person who has spent years in a toxic relationship. Despite the unhappiness, they may stay because they've invested so much time and energy into it. The thought of ending the relationship feels like losing all that effort, even though staying causes ongoing pain.

2.Identity and Self-Worth

Our sense of identity and self-worth can be closely tied to our attachments. If we define ourselves by our job, relationships, or achievements, letting go of these can feel like losing a part of ourselves. This identity attachment makes it difficult to move on, as it challenges our self-concept.

- **Example**: An athlete who defines their worth through their sport might struggle with retirement. Letting go of their career means redefining their identity and finding new sources of self-worth.

Research Insight: The Benefits of Letting Go

While letting go can be challenging, research indicates that it is crucial for psychological and physical well-being. Studies show that those who successfully let go of past grievances and attachments experience lower levels of stress and improved health.

1.Psychological Benefits

A study in the *Journal of Positive Psychology* found that practicing mindfulness and emotional release can lead to significant improvements in mood, stress levels, and overall mental health. Participants who engaged in regular mindfulness practices reported lower levels of anxiety and depression.

2.Physical Health Benefits

Chronic stress from holding onto emotional pain is linked to various physical health issues, including cardiovascular problems and weakened immune function. Letting go reduces stress, which can lead to better physical health outcomes.

- **Research**: A study published in *Health Psychology* demonstrated that individuals who practiced stress-reducing techniques like meditation had lower levels of cortisol, the stress hormone, and better overall health markers.

Sarah's Journey to Let Go of Career Expectations

Sarah's story illustrates the transformative power of letting go of rigid career expectations. As a teacher, Sarah had always envisioned herself as a principal. When setbacks and obstacles prevented her from reaching that goal, she struggled with feelings of inadequacy and failure.

Attending a mindfulness retreat helped Sarah realize that her self-worth wasn't tied to a specific job title. By letting go of the rigid expectations she had placed on herself, Sarah found joy in her role as a teacher and discovered new ways to contribute to her profession. Her journey highlights how releasing the need to adhere to a specific career path can lead to greater fulfillment and personal growth.

Exercise: Reframing the Narrative

Reframing helps shift our perspective on past experiences, turning perceived losses into opportunities for growth. This exercise guides readers through the process of viewing their situation from a new angle.

1. **Identify the Issue**: Write down an event or situation you're struggling to let go of, such as a past relationship or missed opportunity.
2. **Acknowledge the Emotional Attachment**: Note why it's hard to let go—what fears or emotions are attached to it?
3. **Reframe the Situation**: Reflect on how this situation has contributed to your personal growth. What lessons have you learned? How has it prepared you for future opportunities?
4. **Write a New Story**: Create a new narrative where you've let go of the past and are moving forward with clarity. Focus

on how this shift has positively impacted your life.

Rewiring the Brain for Letting Go

Letting go is an ongoing process that requires us to confront and rewire our psychological barriers. By understanding the brain's resistance to change and learning to reframe our attachments, we can start to release the past and embrace a future filled with potential. This chapter lays the groundwork for developing strategies to help you let go and move forward with a renewed sense of purpose and peace.

3

Chapter 3: Embracing Change: How to Navigate Transitions with Grace

The Nature of Change and Transition

Change is an inevitable part of life, yet it often comes with a blend of excitement and anxiety. From career shifts to personal transformations, navigating transitions requires adaptability and resilience. This chapter explores how to embrace change, manage transitions effectively, and turn challenges into opportunities for growth.

Julia's Career Shift

Julia had always been passionate about graphic design, but after ten years in a high-pressure corporate job, she felt burned out. Deciding to pursue her passion full-time, Julia left her stable job to start her own design studio. The transition was filled with uncertainty and fear. She faced financial instability, self-doubt, and the challenge of building a client base from scratch.

Julia's journey is a testament to the power of embracing change. Through networking, continual learning, and a willingness to adapt, she gradually built a successful business. Julia's story highlights the importance of resilience and flexibility in navigating life's transitions.

The Psychology of Change: Understanding Our Reactions

Change triggers a variety of emotional responses, from excitement to fear. Understanding these reactions can help us manage transitions more effectively.

1) The Change Curve

The Change Curve, developed by psychiatrist Elisabeth Kübler-Ross, outlines the stages people go through during change: denial, anger, bargaining, depression, and acceptance. Recognizing where you are on the curve can help you navigate your emotions and develop strategies to move through each stage.

- **Research Insight**: A study in the *Journal of Organizational Behavior* found that understanding the Change Curve can improve employees' adaptability during organizational changes, leading to better outcomes.

2) Fear of the Unknown

Change often involves stepping into the unknown, which can trigger fear and anxiety. This fear is a natural response to uncertainty, but it can be managed with proactive strategies and a positive mindset.

- **Case Study**: A longitudinal study published in *American Psychologist* found that individuals who anticipated change with a positive outlook were more likely to experience successful outcomes compared to those who approached change with fear.

3) Resilience and Adaptability

Resilience—the ability to bounce back from adversity—is crucial for managing change. Developing resilience involves building coping skills, maintaining a positive outlook, and learning from setbacks.

- **Example**: A study in *The Resilience Journal* demonstrated that individuals who practiced resilience-building techniques, such as mindfulness and cognitive restructuring, had better outcomes during periods of change.

Turning Transitions into Opportunities

Transitions, while challenging, can also present valuable opportunities for growth and development. Embracing these opportunities requires a shift in perspective and a proactive approach.

1.Reframe the Transition

Reframing involves changing your perspective on the transition. Instead of viewing it as a setback, see it as an opportunity for growth. This shift in mindset can help you approach the transition with enthusiasm rather than apprehension.

- **Story**: When James lost his job in a corporate downsizing, he initially felt devastated. However, he chose to view the transition as an opportunity to explore his entrepreneurial interests. He started a consulting business, which eventually led to greater fulfillment and success than his previous job.

2.Set New Goals

Use the transition as a chance to set new goals and pursue new passions. Reflect on what you want to achieve in this new phase of your life and create a plan to reach those goals.

- **Exercise**: Create a vision board outlining your goals and aspirations for the transition. Include images, quotes, and milestones that represent your desired outcomes. Use this board as a visual reminder of your objectives and motivations.

3.Build a Support Network

Surround yourself with a supportive network of friends, family, and mentors who can offer guidance, encouragement, and perspective during the transition. Building connections with others who have navigated similar changes can provide valuable insights and support.

- **Story**: After Rachel transitioned from a corporate career to a non-profit organization, she joined a professional group of individuals with similar interests. This network provided her with support, advice, and opportunities to collaborate on meaningful projects.

Practical Strategies for Navigating Transitions

Effective management of transitions involves practical strategies and tools to help you stay on track and maintain balance.

1.Create a Transition Plan

Develop a detailed plan for navigating the transition. Outline the steps you need to take, set milestones, and establish a timeline. Having a clear plan can reduce anxiety and provide a sense of direction.

- **Template**: Use a transition planning template to map out key activities, deadlines, and resources. Include sections for short-term and long-term goals, as well as potential challenges and solutions.

2.Practice Self-Care

During transitions, it's important to prioritize self-care. Engage in activities that promote physical, emotional, and mental well-being. Regular exercise, healthy eating, and relaxation techniques can help you manage stress and maintain a positive outlook.

- **Exercise**: Incorporate self-care routines into your daily schedule. Create a list of activities that help you relax and recharge, such as meditation, journaling, or taking a walk in nature.

3.Seek Professional Guidance

Consider seeking guidance from a career coach, therapist, or mentor to help you navigate the transition. Professional support can provide valuable insights, strategies, and encouragement.

- **Research**: A study in the *Journal of Career Assessment* found that individuals who worked with career coaches during transitions reported higher levels of satisfaction and success compared to those who did not seek professional support.

Emma's Journey Through Personal Transformation

Emma, a 35-year-old teacher, decided to pursue a major life change by going back to school for a graduate degree while working full-time. The transition was challenging, requiring her to balance work, study, and personal life. Emma initially struggled with feelings of overwhelm and self-doubt.

Through careful planning, goal setting, and support from her family and friends, Emma successfully completed her degree. The transition not only enhanced her career prospects but also provided her with a renewed sense of purpose and confidence. Emma's story illustrates how embracing change and proactively managing transitions can lead to profound personal and professional growth.

Exercise: The Transition Toolkit

Create a toolkit to support yourself through the transition. This toolkit should include:

1. **Goal Setting Worksheet**: Outline your goals for the transition and the steps you need to take to achieve them.
2. **Support Network List**: Identify individuals who can provide support and guidance. Include contact information and ways they can help.
3. **Self-Care Plan**: Develop a self-care routine to ensure you maintain balance and well-being during the transition.
4. **Reflection Journal**: Keep a journal to document your experiences, challenges, and successes throughout the transition. Reflect on your progress and any adjustments you need to make.

Navigating Change with Confidence

Navigating transitions with grace involves understanding the psychology of change, embracing new opportunities, and employing practical strategies. By reframing transitions as opportunities for growth, setting clear goals, and seeking support, you can manage change effectively and move forward with confidence. This chapter provides the tools and insights needed to turn life's transitions into pathways for personal and professional development.

4

Chapter 4: The Power of Forgiveness: Healing Through Release

The Healing Journey

Forgiveness often feels like a distant concept when we're hurt or wronged. It's frequently misunderstood as an act of condoning or forgetting past wrongs. However, the essence of forgiveness lies in self-liberation. By choosing to forgive, we release ourselves from the burdens of anger, resentment, and pain. This chapter explores how embracing forgiveness, both towards others and ourselves, can lead to profound emotional healing and personal growth.

Emma's Journey: A Story of Redemption

Emma's tale begins with a significant betrayal. Her once-trusted business partner had undermined her trust, causing both financial losses and emotional distress. For years, Emma clung to her anger, which seeped into her interactions and relationships, creating a cloud of negativity around her.

It wasn't until Emma attended a meditation retreat that she began to understand the impact of her grudges. During a guided meditation session focused on forgiveness, Emma realized that her anger was like a heavy anchor, holding her back from moving forward. The retreat facilitated a profound shift in her perspective. By choosing to forgive, Emma didn't erase the pain but liberated herself from its continuous grip. This act of forgiveness allowed her to heal, rebuild her career, and rekindle her passion for life. Emma's story illustrates the transformative power of forgiveness and its role in reclaiming personal peace.

The Inner Work of Forgiveness

Understanding Emotional Triggers Our emotional triggers are often the remnants of unresolved issues that resurface when we least expect them. These triggers can obstruct our path to forgiveness, keeping us tethered to past wounds. Recognizing and understanding these triggers is crucial for moving past the hurt.

Take Carla's experience, for example. When her ex-partner showed up at her favorite café, Carla felt an intense surge of anger and sadness. This reaction was not just about the encounter but about deeper, unresolved feelings of betrayal. By reflecting on these emotional triggers through journaling and introspection, Carla began to unravel the layers of her pain, which helped her take significant steps towards forgiveness.

The Role of Empathy Empathy allows us to view a situation from another's perspective, which can be a crucial step in the forgiveness process. It's not about justifying the wrongs done to us but understanding the human flaws behind those actions.

Consider the story of Tom and Lisa, whose friendship ended in a heated argument. Tom, feeling the weight of their broken relationship, took the initiative to understand Lisa's viewpoint. He learned about the stress and pressures she was facing at the time of their argument. This act of empathy did not erase the hurt but opened the door to healing and reconciliation. Their renewed understanding led to a deeper, more resilient friendship, showing how empathy can bridge gaps and foster forgiveness.

Forgiveness and Emotional Health: What the Research Says

Research underscores the profound impact of forgiveness on our emotional and physical well-being. Embracing forgiveness can lead to significant improvements in both our mental and physical health.

Reduced Stress and Anxiety Forgiveness is linked to lower levels of stress and anxiety. A study published in *The Journal of Clinical Psychology* explored forgiveness interventions and found that participants who engaged in forgiveness exercises reported a significant reduction in stress and anxiety symptoms. The process of letting go allowed them to experience a greater sense of peace and well-being.

Improved Relationships Forgiveness can enhance our relationships by fostering healthier interactions and deeper connections. Research in *Social Science & Medicine* highlights that individuals who practice forgiveness tend to have more fulfilling and positive relationships. By letting go of past grievances, we create space for empathy, understanding, and mutual respect.

Enhanced Physical Health Chronic anger and resentment can negatively impact physical health, contributing to conditions such as high blood pressure and cardiovascular disease. By practicing forgiveness, individuals can mitigate these health risks. A study in *Health Psychology* found that people who engaged in forgiveness exercises showed lower blood pressure and improved overall health compared to those who did not.

Reflections on Self-Forgiveness

A Journey Through Guilt Self-forgiveness can be particularly challenging due to feelings of guilt and self-blame. Guilt often serves as an emotional barrier to self-forgiveness, keeping us stuck in a cycle of regret and self-punishment.

David's story provides insight into this struggle. After failing to meet a personal commitment, David was overwhelmed with guilt. This guilt clouded his ability to move forward. Through therapy and self-compassion exercises, David learned to address his guilt constructively. He practiced self-forgiveness by acknowledging his mistake, learning from it, and giving himself permission to move forward without lingering self-blame.

The Practice of Self-Compassion Self-compassion involves treating ourselves with kindness and understanding, much like we would for a friend. It's a critical component of self-forgiveness and emotional healing. By practicing self-compassion, we can address our mistakes with a gentler perspective and foster a more forgiving relationship with ourselves.

Lila's experience illustrates this practice. After making a significant mistake at work, Lila found solace in self-compassion exercises. She wrote a letter to herself, acknowledging her humanity and imperfections. This practice helped Lila forgive herself and approach her work with renewed positivity and resilience.

Practical Exercise: The Forgiveness Letter

Writing a forgiveness letter can be a powerful tool for emotional release and healing. This exercise allows you to process your feelings and articulate your decision to forgive.

Steps:

- **Find a Quiet Space**: Choose a calm and private setting where you can reflect without distractions.
- **Write Openly**: Address the letter to the person who has wronged you or to yourself. Express your feelings honestly, detailing how the situation has affected you.
- **Acknowledge the Pain**: Recognize the pain and hurt you've experienced. Validate your emotions without judgment.
- **Express Forgiveness**: Clearly state your decision to forgive. Focus on the liberation this forgiveness brings rather than excusing the behavior.
- **Decide on the Letter's Fate**: After writing, decide whether to send the letter or keep it as a personal reflection. The act of writing is often sufficient for emotional release.

The Forgiveness Ritual: A Symbolic Release

In addition to the forgiveness letter, consider incorporating a symbolic ritual into your forgiveness practice. This ritual could involve creating a physical representation of your emotional release.

The Ritual:

- **Create a Forgiveness Symbol**: Choose an object that represents your emotional burden—such as a stone or a piece of paper.
- **Perform a Release Ceremony**: Find a meaningful way to release this symbol. For example, you might write your grievances on the piece of paper and then burn it, or you could drop the stone into a body of water, symbolizing the release of your emotional weight.
- **Reflect and Move Forward**: Take a moment to reflect on the symbolism of the ritual and the act of letting go. Use this as a stepping stone to move forward with a renewed sense of freedom and peace.

Embracing the Freedom of Forgiveness

Forgiveness is a profound journey of inner liberation and self-discovery. By choosing to forgive ourselves and others, we unlock the door to emotional healing and personal growth. This chapter invites you to explore the transformative power of forgiveness, encouraging you to release past grievances and embrace a future filled with peace and clarity. Remember, forgiveness is not about forgetting but about freeing yourself from the chains of past hurt.

5

Chapter 5: Emotional Boundaries: The Art of Protecting Your Inner Space

Opening Reflection: The Invisible Walls We Build

Imagine walking through a park where every person you meet hands you a heavy rock. At first, you think, "I can carry this." But as more people give you rocks, your load becomes unbearable. This is what happens when we fail to set emotional boundaries—our inner space becomes overloaded with the emotions, expectations, and problems of others.

In this chapter, we'll explore how emotional boundaries serve as invisible walls, protecting our inner peace while allowing healthy connections with others. We'll also examine the consequences of weak or non-existent boundaries and how establishing them can transform relationships, boost self-esteem, and enhance emotional resilience.

Jacob's Struggle with Saying No

Jacob was always the helpful one in his group of friends. Anytime someone needed a favor—whether it was covering a shift at work, lending money, or being a shoulder to cry on—Jacob was there. Over time, though, he began to feel resentful. His time wasn't his own, and he often felt overwhelmed by everyone else's needs.

One afternoon, Jacob found himself sitting in a coffee shop, staring at his phone. His friend Matt had just asked him for another favor, and Jacob felt the familiar weight of obligation. "Why can't I say no?" he thought. Jacob realized that his constant willingness to help had blurred the lines between his responsibilities and those of others. His emotional and mental well-being were suffering.

This turning point led Jacob to explore the concept of emotional boundaries. He started small—saying no to small requests and learning to communicate his limits. Gradually, he reclaimed control over his life, found time for himself, and became more intentional in how he offered help to others. His relationships improved, and his stress levels dropped. Jacob's journey is a reminder that boundaries are not walls to shut others out but doors to let the right people in while maintaining balance.

What Are Emotional Boundaries?

Emotional boundaries are invisible lines that protect your feelings and mental well-being. They define where your emotions end and someone else's begin, allowing you to engage in healthy, balanced relationships.

Without boundaries, you become emotionally drained, stressed, and resentful. But when boundaries are clear, they empower you to engage in meaningful interactions without sacrificing your well-being.

Research Insight: The Psychology of Boundaries

Psychological research highlights the importance of boundaries for emotional well-being. A study in the *Journal of Personality and Social Psychology* emphasizes that people who maintain healthy boundaries report higher levels of self-esteem and lower levels of stress and anxiety. The research shows that emotional boundaries are essential for avoiding "compassion fatigue," which occurs when empathy for others becomes overwhelming and damaging to one's own emotional health.

Furthermore, research conducted by Dr. Brené Brown emphasizes that setting boundaries is a key component of whole-hearted living. Brown's studies have shown that people who are clear about their boundaries experience less resentment and deeper connections with others. Instead of fearing conflict, they embrace boundaries as a form of self-respect.

Interactive Exercise: Identifying Your Emotional Threshold

Understanding your emotional boundaries requires introspection. Take a moment to reflect on situations where you felt drained, overwhelmed, or taken advantage of. These are likely signs that your boundaries were crossed. Try this exercise:

1. **Recall a Recent Event**: Think of a recent interaction where

you felt uncomfortable or resentful afterward. Write down the details.

2. **Analyze Your Feelings**: How did the situation make you feel? Were you frustrated, anxious, or exhausted? Be specific.

3. **Identify the Boundary Violation**: What personal need or limit was ignored in that situation? Did you feel obligated to say yes when you wanted to say no? Were you pressured to provide emotional support at the expense of your own well-being?

4. **Reframe for the Future**: Now, imagine how you could have responded differently. What boundary could you have set? How can you communicate your needs in similar situations moving forward?

This reflective exercise helps to pinpoint where your boundaries need reinforcement.

Case Study: Emotional Boundaries in Relationships

Meet Sarah and Greg. Sarah was deeply empathetic and always wanted to be there for Greg, who struggled with anxiety. Initially, she spent hours on the phone comforting him, often neglecting her own needs in the process. Over time, Sarah became emotionally exhausted. She found herself resenting Greg, though she still cared about him.

After seeking therapy, Sarah learned about emotional boundaries. Her therapist helped her see that while it was important to support Greg, it was equally important to protect her own emotional health. Sarah began setting boundaries by limiting late-night calls and scheduling time for herself. She also communicated her needs to Greg, explaining that she wanted to be supportive but needed balance.

Interestingly, Greg responded positively. Once Sarah set boundaries, their relationship improved. Greg became more self-reliant, and Sarah felt emotionally recharged, allowing her to support him in a healthier way.

Types of Emotional Boundaries

Emotional boundaries come in various forms, each important for maintaining mental and emotional health. Let's explore some key types:

1. **Time Boundaries** Your time is valuable. Time boundaries involve protecting your schedule and energy by not overcommitting. This might mean learning to say no when you're already stretched thin or creating designated "you" time, free from distractions or obligations.

Example: Hannah, a busy lawyer, learned to implement time boundaries by blocking out specific hours each week for self-care. This made her more focused at work and improved her overall well-being.

2. **Emotional Energy Boundaries** These boundaries protect your emotional resources. When someone frequently offloads their problems onto you without reciprocating emotional support, it can drain your energy. Establishing emotional energy boundaries means limiting how much emotional labor you provide

and recognizing when to step back.

Example: John realized that his friendship with David was emotionally exhausting because David often vented about his issues without offering support in return. By creating distance, John preserved his emotional energy and maintained a healthier friendship.

3. Physical Boundaries (Emotional Context) Physical boundaries aren't just about physical space; they also encompass the emotional comfort you feel in proximity to others. These boundaries may involve touch, personal space, or how comfortable you are sharing personal emotions in different settings.

Example: Dana was uncomfortable with how her colleague frequently initiated personal conversations in the middle of the workday. Setting a boundary allowed her to separate work and personal life, reducing stress.

Common Boundary Challenges and Solutions

Challenge 1: Guilt in Setting Boundaries Many people feel guilty for setting boundaries, especially if they are people-pleasers. The fear of disappointing others often leads to sacrificing personal well-being.

Solution: Reframe your understanding of boundaries. Remember that setting a boundary is an act of self-respect, not selfishness. Boundaries allow you to engage more fully and positively in relationships.

Challenge 2: Fear of Conflict Setting boundaries can sometimes lead to uncomfortable conversations or conflicts, which many people avoid.

Solution: Approach boundary-setting with kindness and clarity. Use "I" statements to express your needs without blaming others. For example, "I need some alone time after work to decompress," is more effective than, "You never give me space!"

Research Findings: Boundaries and Mental Health

Dr. Henry Cloud, co-author of *Boundaries: When to Say Yes, How to Say No to Take Control of Your Life*, found that people who establish clear boundaries are more likely to experience emotional stability and healthier interpersonal relationships. In addition, research from *Psychology Today* highlights that boundary-setting is crucial for avoiding emotional burnout and fostering long-term resilience.

Practical Exercise: Role-Playing Boundary Conversations

Setting boundaries can feel intimidating, especially if you're not used to it. This role-playing exercise can help you prepare for real-life situations where boundary-setting is necessary.

1. **Choose a Boundary Scenario**: Think of a common scenario where you struggle to set boundaries. This could be with a colleague, friend, or family member.
2. **Write a Boundary Statement**: Draft a clear and respectful statement that communicates your boundary. For example,

"I appreciate your desire to spend time together, but I need some time alone to recharge."

3. **Practice Aloud**: Stand in front of a mirror or ask a friend to role-play with you. Practice saying your boundary statement confidently and calmly.
4. **Reflect**: After practicing, reflect on how you feel. Does the boundary statement feel authentic to you? What fears or anxieties arise, and how can you address them?

Protecting Your Inner Space

Emotional boundaries are a form of self-care. By establishing clear limits on your emotional, mental, and physical space, you protect your inner peace and engage in healthier, more balanced relationships. Boundaries allow you to live authentically, free from the weight of other people's expectations and demands. As you continue to explore and implement boundaries, remember that this is an ongoing process—one that will empower you to live with greater clarity, confidence, and emotional well-being.

6

Chapter 6: Overcoming Resistance: The Roadblocks to Letting Go

Why Is Letting Go So Hard?

Take a moment and think about something you've been holding onto for far too long. It might be a grudge, a past mistake, or an old relationship. Now, ask yourself: *Why am I still holding on? What is it that makes letting go feel so impossible at times?*

Letting go is one of the hardest emotional challenges we face, yet it's essential for growth and peace. The key to mastering the art of letting go lies in understanding the roadblocks that keep us stuck. In this chapter, we'll dive into the most common forms of resistance—fear, attachment, and comfort—and explore how you can overcome them to finally free yourself from emotional baggage.

Daniel's Dilemma – Holding Onto the "What Ifs"

Daniel had been out of his last relationship for nearly three years, yet he found himself constantly revisiting old memories, wondering, *What if things had gone differently?* His ex was long gone, but in his mind, the relationship was alive and well. Every new romantic possibility was overshadowed by the lingering "what ifs."

For Daniel, the problem wasn't the breakup itself, but his attachment to the future he had imagined with his ex. He wasn't just holding on to a person—he was holding on to a version of his life that no longer existed.

One day, Daniel's therapist asked him a simple question: *What would letting go give you that holding on never could?* This question struck him deeply. By holding onto the "what ifs," Daniel was missing out on new opportunities, new relationships, and, most importantly, his own happiness.

Through counseling and self-reflection, Daniel slowly let go of the imagined future. He began to live in the present and embrace the possibilities ahead. His story is a perfect example of how our minds create resistance by holding onto the past, even when we know it's time to move on.

Interactive Reflection: What Are You Still Holding Onto?

Take a moment to reflect on your own life. Is there something or someone you've been holding onto that you know deep down it's time to release? Answer these questions to help guide your reflection:

1. **What's the one thing you've been unable to let go of?** Is it

a past relationship, a mistake, or an unfulfilled dream?

2. **What fears or emotions come up when you think about letting go?** Is it fear of the unknown, worry about failure, or sadness over what's lost?

3. **What would your life look like if you did let go?** Imagine the freedom and peace you might feel. What new opportunities could arise?

Jot down your thoughts, even if they feel incomplete. This exercise is the first step in identifying your own resistance.

The Fear Factor: Why Letting Go Feels Risky

Let's talk about fear. If you're having trouble letting go, chances are fear is playing a big role. Fear of failure, fear of uncertainty, fear of losing control—it all bubbles up when we face the unknown.

The thing about fear is that it tricks us into believing that holding onto the past is safer than embracing the future. But here's the truth: The future is uncertain whether you hold on or let go. The only difference is, when you let go, you make space for new things to enter your life.

Case Study: Fear of the Unknown – Maria's Career Decision

Maria worked at a job that she no longer loved. Every morning, she dreaded going to the office, but the idea of quitting filled her with anxiety. What if she couldn't find another job? What if she failed at something new? So, she stayed, trapped by the fear of the unknown.

One day, Maria read an article about career transitions that struck a chord with her. It said, *"Staying in a place where you're not growing is more risky than stepping into the unknown."* This realization hit her hard. Maria understood that by staying in a job she hated, she was stalling her own growth and potential happiness. She took small steps at first—updating her resume, exploring other fields, and eventually applying for new jobs.

Within six months, Maria had left her old job and found a new position that aligned with her passions. Letting go of her fear of failure opened doors she hadn't even considered.

Breaking Free from Attachment: Why We Cling to the Familiar

It's human nature to cling to what's familiar, even when it no longer serves us. Whether it's a toxic relationship, an old habit, or outdated beliefs, attachment often feels like a security blanket.

But here's the kicker: what feels familiar isn't always good for us. In fact, many of the things we cling to are the very things keeping us stuck in a cycle of unhappiness.

Interactive Prompt: Are You Stuck in Attachment? Think of one area in your life where you feel stuck. Maybe it's a relationship, a job, or even a mindset. Ask yourself:

- **Why am I still holding on to this?** Is it because it's familiar, or because it's truly adding value to my life?
- **What would happen if I let go of this attachment?** Would it lead to discomfort, or could it open up new possibilities?

Write down your answers. Reflect on whether your attachment is driven by comfort or by genuine need.

Comfort Zones: The Silent Enemy of Growth

Comfort zones are deceptive. They lull us into a state of false security, making us believe that staying put is easier than pushing forward. But staying in your comfort zone means one thing—no growth.

You know the feeling: You've wanted to make a change, but the thought of discomfort—whether it's emotional, financial, or physical—keeps you anchored to the same spot. The problem is, comfort zones are like quicksand. The longer you stay, the harder it becomes to get out.

Kelly's Comfort Zone Trap Kelly had been in a long-term relationship that was stagnant. She and her partner no longer shared the same goals, and while they weren't fighting, they weren't growing together either. But breaking up seemed terrifying. They had built a life together, shared mutual friends, and the idea of being alone was frightening.

For years, Kelly stayed in the relationship, convincing herself that "good enough" was better than the discomfort of starting over. Then, one evening, while watching a documentary on self-growth, Kelly heard a quote that shook her: *"If you're not growing, you're dying. There's no standing still in life."* This resonated deeply with her. She realized that staying in the relationship was keeping both of them from finding the happiness they deserved.

Eventually, Kelly found the courage to leave. The months following the breakup were tough, filled with moments of doubt and loneliness, but they were also filled with growth. She rediscovered who she was outside of the relationship, made new connections, and opened herself to new possibilities. Kelly's story illustrates the trap of comfort zones and the rewards that await when we dare to step outside them.

Overcoming Resistance: A Plan of Action

It's time to take action! You've read the stories, reflected on your own resistance, and now it's time to break free. The following exercises are designed to help you challenge your resistance and make real progress toward letting go.

Interactive Exercise: The Fear-Reality Check

One powerful way to confront your fears is to challenge their validity. Often, our fears are exaggerated versions of reality. Here's an exercise to help you see things more clearly:

1. **Write down your biggest fear** related to letting go. For example, "I'm afraid I'll fail if I try something new."
2. **Ask yourself: What's the worst that could happen?** Be honest but not dramatic. Consider the real consequences of your fear.
3. **Now, write the best-case scenario.** If everything went well, what could you gain from letting go? What new opportunities could arise?
4. **Reflect on the middle ground.** The reality of most situations lies somewhere between our worst and best-case

scenarios. Write a realistic outcome of letting go, factoring in both the challenges and the potential rewards.

This exercise helps you put your fears into perspective and empowers you to make decisions based on reality, not exaggerated anxieties.

Exercise: 30-Day Letting Go Challenge

This challenge is designed to get you out of your comfort zone and actively practicing the art of letting go.

- **Week 1: Declutter Your Space** – Start by letting go of physical clutter. Clean out your closet, donate old items, and create space in your environment. You'll be surprised how much lighter you feel when your surroundings reflect openness.
- **Week 2: Let Go of a Negative Habit** – Identify one habit that no longer serves you. It could be procrastination, negative self-talk, or an unhealthy routine. Replace it with a positive action.
- **Week 3: Release an Emotional Grudge** – Focus on one emotional grudge or resentment you've been holding onto. Write a letter expressing your feelings (you don't have to send it), and commit to releasing that anger or hurt.
- **Week 4: Challenge Your Comfort Zone** – Do one thing that scares you. It could be as simple as having a difficult conversation or as big as taking the first step toward a life goal. The goal is to practice stepping outside your comfort zone and embracing uncertainty.

The Power of Release

Letting go isn't a one-time decision—it's a lifelong practice. But with each step you take, you'll find that the weight of your past gets lighter, your fears less daunting, and your path forward clearer. Overcoming resistance takes time, patience, and courage, but once you start, you'll see that freedom and growth are waiting just beyond the walls you've built.

By engaging in these exercises, reflecting on your own resistance, and making small steps forward, you can break free from the past and open yourself to the endless possibilities of the future.

7

Chapter 7: Emotional Reframing: Shifting Perspectives to Transform Your Life

The Power of Perspective

Imagine looking through a pair of glasses with tinted lenses. Everything you see is colored by those lenses, altering your perception of reality. Now, picture what happens if you change those lenses to a different color or remove them entirely. Your view of the world shifts dramatically.

In the same way, emotional reframing involves changing how we perceive our experiences to alter our emotional responses. It's about shifting from a negative or limiting viewpoint to one that fosters growth, resilience, and positivity. This chapter explores how reframing can transform your life by changing the way you interpret events and emotions.

Mia's New Lens

Mia had always been a perfectionist. Every mistake, no matter how small, felt like a personal failure. This constant self-criticism led to stress, anxiety, and a lack of satisfaction in her achievements. She felt trapped in a cycle of high expectations and disappointment.

One day, Mia's mentor shared a story about a renowned artist who viewed mistakes as opportunities for creativity. This perspective shift was a revelation for Mia. Instead of seeing her errors as failures, she started to view them as chances to learn and grow.

Mia began practicing this new mindset in her daily life. When she made a mistake at work, she asked herself, *What can I learn from this?* This reframing allowed her to approach challenges with curiosity rather than fear. Over time, Mia's stress decreased, and her sense of accomplishment increased. Her story illustrates the profound impact of reframing on personal growth and emotional well-being.

The Science of Reframing: How It Works

Emotional reframing is grounded in cognitive behavioral therapy (CBT), a well-established psychological approach that focuses on changing negative thought patterns. Research from the *Journal of Cognitive Psychotherapy* shows that reframing helps individuals shift their perspective, leading to reduced stress and improved emotional health.

Key Findings:

- **Cognitive Flexibility:** Studies indicate that reframing increases cognitive flexibility, allowing individuals to view situations from multiple angles. This flexibility is associated with better problem-solving skills and emotional resilience.
- **Stress Reduction:** Research in *Health Psychology* shows that individuals who practice reframing experience lower levels of stress and anxiety. By altering their perception of stressful situations, they can manage their responses more effectively.

Interactive Exercise: Reframe Your Recent Challenge

Let's apply reframing to a recent challenge you've faced. This exercise will help you practice shifting your perspective.

1. **Identify a Recent Challenge**: Think of a situation that caused you stress or frustration recently. Write down a brief description of the event.
2. **Current Perspective**: Describe how you currently view this situation. What negative thoughts or feelings are associated with it?
3. **Alternative Perspectives**: Brainstorm at least three different ways to view this situation. For example, if you're stressed about a missed deadline, consider perspectives such as "This is an opportunity to improve my time management skills" or "Missing this deadline has taught me the importance of better planning."
4. **Choose a New Frame**: Select one of the alternative perspectives that feels most empowering or constructive. Write down how adopting this new frame changes your emotional response to the situation.

5. **Action Plan**: Based on your new perspective, outline one actionable step you can take to address the situation or improve your response moving forward.

This exercise helps in practicing reframing by turning negative experiences into opportunities for growth.

John's Job Search – From Defeat to Opportunity

John had been job hunting for months without success. Each rejection letter felt like a personal blow, and his self-esteem took a hit. He started doubting his abilities and feared he'd never find the right job.

John's career coach introduced him to reframing techniques. Instead of viewing each rejection as a failure, John began to see them as steps in the learning process. He started asking for feedback from each interview, using the information to refine his approach.

John's shift in perspective led to increased confidence and a more proactive approach to his job search. Within a few months, he secured a position that was not only a good fit for his skills but also aligned with his career goals. John's story highlights how reframing setbacks can transform a challenging situation into a valuable learning experience and eventual success.

Common Reframing Techniques

Here are some practical reframing techniques you can use to change your perspective and improve your emotional response:

1. **Positive Reinterpretation:** This involves finding a positive angle in a seemingly negative situation. For instance, if you didn't get the job you wanted, reinterpret it as a chance to explore other opportunities that might be a better fit.

2. **Perspective-Taking:** Consider how someone else might view the same situation. This can provide insights into alternative ways to perceive the event. For example, how would a mentor or friend view your current challenge?

3. **Gratitude Reframing:** Focus on what you can be grateful for in a difficult situation. This could involve recognizing the growth opportunities or support systems you have, even when things are tough.

4. **Self-Compassion:** Reframe self-criticism by practicing self-compassion. Instead of harshly judging yourself for a mistake, treat yourself with the same kindness you would offer a friend in a similar situation.

Interactive Exercise: Perspective-Taking Journaling

Journaling can help deepen your practice of reframing. Use the following prompts to explore different perspectives on a challenging situation:

Describe the Situation: Write a detailed account of the situation you're facing.

Current Thoughts: Note down your initial thoughts and feelings about the situation.

Different Perspectives:

- **A Mentor's View**: Imagine what advice your mentor would give you about this situation.
- **A Friend's View**: Consider how a close friend might interpret or handle the situation.
- **Your Future Self's View**: Reflect on how you'll look back on this situation a year from now. How might it appear different in retrospect?

New Insights: Summarize any new insights or perspectives you've gained from this exercise. How might these insights help you approach the situation differently?

The Role of Self-Talk in Reframing

Self-talk plays a crucial role in how we perceive and respond to situations. Positive self-talk can reinforce new perspectives, while negative self-talk can perpetuate old, limiting beliefs.

Research Insight: A study in *Social Cognitive and Affective Neuroscience* found that individuals who engage in positive self-talk and cognitive reframing have higher levels of psychological well-being and are more resilient to stress.

Practical Tip: Pay attention to your self-talk. When you catch yourself engaging in negative or limiting self-talk, consciously shift to a more positive or constructive perspective. Practice affirmations or encouraging statements to reinforce a new, healthier view.

Embracing the Power of Reframing

Emotional reframing is a powerful tool for transforming how we experience and respond to life's challenges. By shifting your perspective, you can turn obstacles into opportunities, setbacks into lessons, and stress into growth.

Remember, reframing is a skill that improves with practice. The more you consciously apply these techniques, the more natural they will become, leading to a more resilient and positive approach to life's ups and downs.

By embracing reframing, you empower yourself to change your emotional landscape and unlock new possibilities for personal growth and fulfillment.

8

Chapter 8: Building Emotional Resilience: Strategies for Bouncing Back Stronger

What Is Emotional Resilience?

Emotional resilience is akin to a psychological immune system that enables you to withstand and recover from stress, adversity, and trauma. It's not about avoiding challenges but developing the capacity to adapt and emerge stronger. Resilience allows you to bounce back from setbacks and continue forward with renewed strength and insight.

Imagine resilience as a mental muscle. Just as you strengthen physical muscles through exercise, you build emotional resilience through practice and strategies. This chapter is designed to equip you with tools and techniques to enhance this critical aspect of your mental and emotional health.

Interactive Story: Emma's Journey to Resilience

Emma's story is a compelling example of how resilience can be cultivated through intentional effort and mindset shifts. When faced with a series of personal and professional challenges, Emma found herself at a crossroads. Her response to these challenges—focusing on small victories and gratitude—was instrumental in her journey to resilience.

Detailed Breakdown:

- **Daily Goal Setting:** Emma started setting small, achievable goals each day, like taking a walk or completing a work task. These small wins provided a sense of accomplishment and control amidst the chaos.
- **Gratitude Journaling:** By maintaining a gratitude journal, Emma trained her mind to focus on positive aspects of her life, shifting her perspective from what was going wrong to what was going right.
- **Seeking Support:** Emma also reached out to friends and mentors, leveraging her support network to gain encouragement and advice.

These strategies helped Emma build a resilient mindset, enabling her to face future challenges with greater confidence and less stress.

The Science of Resilience: What Research Reveals

Understanding the scientific basis of emotional resilience can deepen your appreciation of its importance and effectiveness. Research has provided valuable insights into the factors that contribute to resilience.

Key Research Findings:

- **Positive Mindset:** The *Journal of Personality and Social Psychology* found that a positive mindset significantly enhances resilience. Those who view challenges as opportunities rather than threats are better equipped to handle stress.
- **Social Support:** According to *American Psychologist*, having a strong support system acts as a buffer against stress. Emotional support from friends, family, or support groups provides reassurance and practical assistance during tough times.
- **Self-Efficacy:** A study in *Psychological Review* highlighted that self-efficacy, or the belief in one's ability to influence outcomes, is crucial for resilience. Individuals with high self-efficacy are more likely to persevere through difficulties and achieve their goals.

By incorporating these research findings into your resilience-building practices, you can develop a more robust and scientifically grounded approach to managing adversity.

Interactive Exercise: Building Your Resilience Toolbox

Creating a resilience toolbox is an empowering way to prepare for and manage challenges. This exercise involves identifying and organizing strategies that will support you in tough times.

Step-by-Step Guide:

1. **Identify Your Strengths:** Reflect on past experiences where you successfully overcame difficulties. List the strengths

and skills you used, such as problem-solving, adaptability, or optimism.

2. **Resilience Strategies:** Write down specific strategies that have helped you cope with stress. These could include mindfulness practices, time management techniques, or creative outlets.

3. **Support Network:** Make a list of people who provide emotional and practical support. Include their contact information and note how they help you, whether through advice, encouragement, or practical assistance.

4. **Self-Care Practices:** Identify activities that replenish your energy and enhance your well-being. This might include exercise, hobbies, or relaxation techniques like meditation or reading.

5. **Action Plan:** Develop a plan for using your resilience toolbox when faced with challenges. For instance, if you encounter a stressful situation, refer to your support network, practice mindfulness, and remind yourself of your strengths.

By organizing these elements, you create a practical resource for managing and enhancing your resilience.

Case Study: Lucas's Resilience in the Face of Adversity

Lucas's journey from struggling entrepreneur to successful business owner demonstrates the power of resilience in transforming adversity into opportunity.

Detailed Breakdown:

- **Initial Setbacks:** Lucas faced several setbacks, including financial difficulties and market rejections. These challenges initially felt overwhelming and discouraging.
- **Strategic Adaptation:** Lucas embraced resilience by viewing setbacks as opportunities to learn and adapt. He sought feedback, adjusted his business strategies, and focused on his strengths.
- **Support System:** Lucas built a network of mentors and advisors who provided guidance and encouragement. Their support was crucial in helping him navigate challenges and stay motivated.
- **Self-Care:** Lucas also prioritized his well-being by incorporating regular exercise and relaxation into his routine. This helped him manage stress and maintain a balanced perspective.

Lucas's story highlights how resilience can turn obstacles into stepping stones, leading to growth and success.

Interactive Exercise: The Resilience Reflection

Reflecting on past experiences where you demonstrated resilience can reinforce your ability to handle future challenges. This exercise helps you gain insights from previous successes.

Step-by-Step Guide:

1. **Recall a Past Challenge:** Think of a significant challenge you faced and overcame. Describe the situation in detail, including your initial thoughts and feelings.
2. **Resilience Factors:** Identify the factors that contributed

to your resilience during this time. Did you use specific strategies, seek support, or maintain a positive outlook?

3. **Lessons Learned:** Reflect on the lessons you learned from this experience. How did it contribute to your personal growth and resilience?

4. **Apply to Current Situation:** Apply these lessons to a current challenge you're facing. Consider how your past experiences can inform your approach and help you navigate the situation.

This exercise allows you to leverage past resilience to address current and future challenges effectively.

Developing Resilience: Practical Strategies

Enhancing your emotional resilience involves integrating practical strategies into your daily life. These strategies support your ability to cope with stress and bounce back from adversity.

1. **Practice Mindfulness:** Mindfulness meditation helps you stay present and reduce stress. By focusing on the present moment, you can manage your emotional responses more effectively and cultivate a sense of calm.

2. **Set Realistic Goals:** Break down large challenges into smaller, manageable goals. This approach makes it easier to tackle problems and track your progress, providing a sense of achievement and motivation.

3. **Build Strong Relationships:** Invest time in nurturing relationships with family, friends, and colleagues. A supportive network provides emotional resources and practical assistance during tough times.

4. **Develop Problem-Solving Skills:** Enhance your ability to address challenges by practicing problem-solving techniques. Approach problems systematically, considering multiple solutions and evaluating their potential outcomes.

5. **Embrace Flexibility:** Be open to change and adapt to new circumstances. Flexibility allows you to navigate uncertainties and recover from setbacks more effectively, fostering resilience.

Interactive Exercise: The Resilience Vision Board

Creating a vision board helps visualize and manifest your resilience goals. This interactive exercise encourages you to set clear intentions and stay focused on your aspirations.

Step-by-Step Guide:

1. **Gather Materials:** Collect magazines, printouts, or digital images that represent your goals and aspirations. You'll also need a board or large paper and glue.

2. **Visualize Your Goals:** Think about areas where you want to build resilience. This could include career goals, personal growth, or health.

3. **Create Your Vision Board:** Cut out images, words, and phrases that symbolize your resilience goals. Arrange them on your board and glue them in place.

4. **Display Your Board:** Place your vision board in a visible location to remind yourself of your goals and motivations.

5. **Review and Reflect:** Regularly review your vision board to stay focused on your aspirations and celebrate your progress. Update it as your goals evolve or new insights

emerge.

The Journey of Resilience

Building emotional resilience is a continuous journey that involves learning, growth, and practice. By incorporating the strategies and exercises from this chapter, you can strengthen your ability to handle adversity and maintain emotional well-being.

Resilience is not about avoiding difficulties but about developing the mindset and skills to navigate them effectively. Embrace the process, stay committed to your growth, and trust in your capacity to overcome challenges.

With resilience, you can transform obstacles into opportunities and face life's ups and downs with greater strength and confidence.

9

Chapter 9: Transforming Setbacks into Opportunities: Turning Adversity into Growth

The Power of Perspective

Have you ever heard the saying, "When life gives you lemons, make lemonade"? It's a reminder that challenges and setbacks can be reframed as opportunities for growth. The way you perceive and respond to adversity plays a crucial role in transforming it into a stepping stone for personal development.

In this chapter, we'll delve into the concept of turning setbacks into opportunities for growth. You'll learn strategies for shifting your perspective, embracing challenges, and using adversity as a catalyst for positive change.

Sarah's Reinvention

Sarah's story exemplifies how setbacks can lead to significant personal and professional growth. After losing her job due to company downsizing, Sarah felt lost and disheartened. However, instead of dwelling on her misfortune, she chose to view the situation as an opportunity for reinvention.

Detailed Breakdown:

- **Reevaluating Goals:** Sarah took time to reflect on her career aspirations and personal interests. She used this period of unemployment to reassess what she truly wanted from her career.
- **Skill Development:** She enrolled in online courses to develop new skills and enhance her expertise in areas she was passionate about. This not only improved her marketability but also reignited her enthusiasm for her work.
- **Networking:** Sarah actively engaged in networking events and connected with professionals in her field. These interactions opened doors to new opportunities and provided valuable insights.

Sarah's proactive approach and willingness to view her setback as a chance for growth ultimately led her to a more fulfilling and rewarding career path.

The Science of Reframing: How Perspective Impacts Growth

Research in psychology highlights the importance of reframing in transforming setbacks into opportunities. Understanding how perspective influences growth can empower you to approach challenges with a constructive mindset.

Key Research Findings:

- **Growth Mindset:** Carol Dweck's research on mindset, as published in *Mindset: The New Psychology of Success*, demonstrates that individuals with a growth mindset—believing that abilities and intelligence can be developed—are more likely to embrace challenges and persist through difficulties.
- **Cognitive Reappraisal:** Studies in *Emotion* journal reveal that cognitive reappraisal, or changing the way you think about a situation, can reduce stress and improve emotional outcomes. By viewing setbacks as opportunities for learning, you can enhance your resilience and well-being.
- **Post-Traumatic Growth:** Research in *Journal of Traumatic Stress* shows that individuals who experience trauma often report personal growth as a result. This phenomenon, known as post-traumatic growth, underscores the potential for significant positive change following adversity.

These findings illustrate how shifting your perspective can turn setbacks into valuable opportunities for growth.

Interactive Exercise: The Adversity Reframe

The Adversity Reframe exercise helps you practice reframing challenges into opportunities for growth. This exercise involves examining a current or past setback and identifying potential positive outcomes.

Step-by-Step Guide:

1. **Identify the Setback:** Think of a recent or past challenge

or setback. Describe the situation in detail, including the impact it had on you.

2. **Reframe the Challenge:** Consider how you might reframe the situation. Ask yourself questions like, "What can I learn from this experience?" or "How can this challenge help me grow?"

3. **Positive Outcomes:** List potential positive outcomes or opportunities that could arise from the challenge. For example, increased resilience, new skills, or personal insights.

4. **Action Plan:** Develop an action plan for leveraging the positive outcomes. Outline specific steps you can take to capitalize on the opportunities identified.

5. **Reflect:** Reflect on how this exercise changes your perspective on the setback. Notice any shifts in your emotional response or attitude toward the challenge.

This exercise encourages you to view setbacks through a lens of opportunity, fostering a mindset of growth and resilience.

Case Study: Tom's Career Transition

Tom's experience demonstrates how a career setback can lead to significant personal and professional growth. After being laid off from his job, Tom initially felt overwhelmed and uncertain about his future. However, he decided to use the setback as an opportunity for reinvention.

Detailed Breakdown:

- **Exploring Passions:** Tom took time to explore his passions and interests, which led him to discover a new career path in a field he had always been interested in but never pursued.

- **Building Skills:** He invested time in acquiring new skills and certifications relevant to his new career path. This not only increased his employability but also boosted his confidence.
- **Entrepreneurial Ventures:** Tom also considered starting his own business, leveraging his skills and expertise to create something meaningful and fulfilling.

Tom's proactive approach and willingness to embrace change resulted in a rewarding career transition and personal growth.

Interactive Exercise: The Opportunity Mapping

Opportunity Mapping helps you identify and explore the potential opportunities arising from a current or past challenge. This exercise involves mapping out the connections between challenges and growth opportunities.

Step-by-Step Guide:

1. **Map the Challenge:** Draw a central circle on a sheet of paper or digital tool. In the center, write the challenge or setback you're facing.
2. **Identify Opportunities:** Surround the central circle with additional circles representing potential opportunities. These opportunities could include personal growth, new skills, or career changes.
3. **Explore Connections:** Connect each opportunity to the central challenge with lines. For each connection, write a brief explanation of how the opportunity relates to or

arises from the challenge.

4. **Action Steps:** For each identified opportunity, list actionable steps you can take to explore or pursue it.

5. **Review and Reflect:** Review your opportunity map and reflect on how it changes your perspective on the challenge. Consider how you can use this information to guide your actions and decisions.

Strategies for Embracing and Leveraging Setbacks

Embracing setbacks and leveraging them for growth involves adopting specific strategies that foster resilience and adaptability.

1. **Embrace a Growth Mindset:** Cultivate a mindset that views challenges as opportunities for learning and growth. Approach setbacks with curiosity and openness, focusing on what you can learn from the experience.

2. **Develop Problem-Solving Skills:** Strengthen your problem-solving abilities by tackling challenges systematically. Break down problems into manageable parts, explore potential solutions, and evaluate their effectiveness.

3. **Seek Feedback and Support:** Engage with mentors, peers, or support groups to gain feedback and perspectives on your challenges. Their insights can help you navigate setbacks and identify opportunities for growth.

4. **Practice Self-Compassion:** Be kind to yourself during difficult times. Acknowledge your efforts and progress, and

avoid self-criticism. Self-compassion fosters resilience and helps you maintain a positive outlook.

5. **Set Incremental Goals:** Break down larger goals into smaller, achievable steps. This approach makes it easier to track progress, maintain motivation, and celebrate small victories along the way.

Interactive Exercise: The Growth Journal

The Growth Journal exercise encourages you to document and reflect on your experiences with setbacks and growth opportunities. This practice helps you track your progress and insights over time.

Step-by-Step Guide:

1. **Journal Entry:** Set aside time each day or week to write a journal entry about recent setbacks and challenges you've faced.
2. **Reflect on Growth:** Reflect on how each challenge has contributed to your personal growth. Note any new skills, insights, or opportunities that have arisen as a result.
3. **Track Progress:** Keep track of your progress in overcoming challenges and leveraging opportunities. Record any achievements, lessons learned, or changes in perspective.
4. **Celebrate Successes:** Regularly review your journal to celebrate your successes and acknowledge your resilience. Use this reflection to motivate and inspire yourself.
5. **Set Future Goals:** Based on your reflections, set future goals for personal and professional growth. Outline steps

you can take to continue leveraging setbacks as opportunities.

Embracing Adversity as a Pathway to Growth

Transforming setbacks into opportunities requires a shift in perspective and a proactive approach to overcoming challenges. By applying the strategies and exercises from this chapter, you can turn adversity into a catalyst for personal growth and development.

Remember, setbacks are not roadblocks but stepping stones on your journey to success. Embrace challenges with a mindset of growth, leverage opportunities for learning, and continue to build resilience. Through this process, you'll discover new strengths and capabilities that drive you forward.

10

Chapter 10: Cultivating a Growth Mindset: How to Develop and Sustain a Mindset for Success

Jenna's Revelation

Imagine Jenna, a talented graphic designer with a dream of becoming a creative director. Despite her skills, she often felt defeated by obstacles and feared failure. It wasn't until she stumbled upon the concept of a growth mindset that her world changed.

Jenna's discovery was a turning point. She learned that a growth mindset—believing that her abilities could be developed through dedication and hard work—was the key to overcoming her self-doubt. This realization was more than just an idea; it was a transformative force that reshaped her approach to challenges.

Michael's Breakthrough

Michael, a software engineer, faced numerous setbacks in his quest for a promotion. He viewed his initial failures as indications of his limitations, believing that some people were just born with leadership qualities. However, Michael's perspective shifted dramatically when he read about Carol Dweck's research on growth mindset.

Michael began experimenting with new approaches. He took on projects that pushed his boundaries, sought feedback with an open mind, and focused on continuous learning. Slowly, his mindset evolved. Challenges that once seemed like insurmountable obstacles became opportunities for growth. His new approach not only improved his technical skills but also significantly boosted his confidence and leadership capabilities.

The Science Behind Growth Mindset

Growth Mindset and Achievement

Carol Dweck's groundbreaking research reveals that individuals with a growth mindset are more likely to achieve their goals. Studies show that people who believe in their ability to improve through effort and learning are more resilient and persistent.

- **Academic Success:** Research published in *Journal of Educational Psychology* indicates that students with a growth mindset perform better academically. They are more likely to embrace challenges and persist through difficulties.
- **Workplace Performance:** In *Psychological Science*, findings suggest that employees with a growth mindset show higher job performance and adaptability. They are more open to

feedback and view failures as learning opportunities.

These insights demonstrate how adopting a growth mindset can positively impact various aspects of life, from education to career advancement.

Shifting Your Perspective

Reflect on a recent challenge you faced. Picture the situation as if you were Jenna or Michael. How would approaching this challenge with a growth mindset change your experience?

Reflective Questions:

- **What Beliefs Held You Back?** Consider the beliefs you had about your abilities or the situation. How did these beliefs influence your response?
- **How Can You Reframe the Challenge?** Think about how adopting a growth mindset might alter your approach. What opportunities for learning and development can you identify?
- **What Actions Can You Take?** Based on your reflections, outline specific actions you can take to embrace a growth mindset. How will these actions help you overcome obstacles and achieve your goals?

Use these reflections to gain insights into how a growth mindset can transform your approach to challenges and foster personal and professional growth.

Interactive Exercise: Growth Mindset Journal

The Growth Mindset Journal exercise is designed to help you track your journey towards developing a growth mindset.

Steps to Follow:

1. **Journal Entry:** Start each journal entry with a description of a challenge or setback you're currently facing or have faced recently.
2. **Mindset Analysis:** Reflect on your initial mindset regarding this challenge. Were your thoughts and beliefs aligned with a growth mindset or a fixed mindset?
3. **Reframe and Reassess:** Reframe the challenge using growth mindset principles. Write down how you can approach the situation differently and what opportunities for growth it presents.
4. **Action Plan:** Create an action plan based on your reflections. List specific steps you can take to implement a growth mindset in this situation.
5. **Review and Reflect:** Regularly review your journal entries to track your progress and insights. Reflect on any changes in your mindset and the impact on your actions and outcomes.

Case Study: Emily's Mindset Makeover

Emily's story provides a compelling example of how embracing a growth mindset can lead to significant personal and professional growth. Working as a marketing manager, Emily initially struggled with public speaking, often avoiding opportunities to present her ideas.

After learning about the growth mindset, Emily decided to tackle her fear head-on. She sought out public speaking workshops, practiced regularly, and welcomed constructive feedback. Over time, Emily's confidence grew, and her speaking skills improved. Her willingness to face challenges and learn from them opened doors to new career opportunities and personal fulfillment.

Emily's journey underscores the power of a growth mindset in overcoming self-imposed limitations and achieving success.

Strategies for Nurturing a Growth Mindset

Building and sustaining a growth mindset involves integrating specific practices into your daily life. These strategies help reinforce a belief in your ability to grow and develop.

- **Embrace Learning Opportunities:** Actively seek out experiences that challenge you and promote learning. Whether it's a new skill, a difficult project, or a complex problem, view these opportunities as chances to expand your abilities.
- **Cultivate Curiosity:** Maintain a curious mindset by exploring new interests and pursuing knowledge. Curiosity drives innovation and helps you approach challenges with enthusiasm and creativity.
- **Seek Feedback and Reflect:** Regularly seek feedback from others and reflect on your experiences. Use feedback as a tool for growth and view reflections as a means of continuous improvement.
- **Celebrate Effort and Progress:** Focus on the effort you invest and the progress you make. Celebrate small victories and recognize the value of persistence and hard work.

- **Practice Self-Compassion:** Be kind to yourself when facing setbacks or challenges. Acknowledge that growth involves making mistakes and learning from them, and approach yourself with compassion and understanding.

Embracing a Growth Mindset for a Brighter Future

Cultivating a growth mindset is a journey of transformation and self-discovery. By embracing challenges, seeking feedback, and celebrating progress, you can develop a mindset that fosters resilience and success.

Remember, a growth mindset is a dynamic approach to learning and development. Continuously nurture this mindset, apply the strategies outlined in this chapter, and watch as you unlock your full potential.

With a growth mindset, you're not just navigating challenges; you're turning them into opportunities for growth and success. Embrace the journey and continue to cultivate a mindset that drives you towards a brighter and more fulfilling future.

11

Embracing the Journey of Self-Discovery and Growth

As we reach the end of our journey through the realms of personal development, it's essential to reflect on the key takeaways and the transformative potential of embracing change and growth. This book has been a guide through various facets of self-discovery, helping you unlock the power within yourself to create a more fulfilling and successful life.

Reflecting on the Journey

Throughout these chapters, we've explored diverse aspects of personal growth, from understanding the power of emotional intelligence to cultivating a growth mindset. Each chapter offered unique insights, interactive exercises, and real-life stories designed to inspire and motivate you.

Think back to the stories of Jenna, Michael, Emily, and others who faced challenges and embraced change. Their journeys are not just inspirational; they are practical illustrations of how applying these principles can lead to profound personal and professional transformation.

Key Takeaways: Empowering Your Growth

As you close this book, consider the following key takeaways:

- **Emotional Intelligence:** Recognize the significance of understanding and managing your emotions and the emotions of others. Emotional intelligence is crucial for building strong relationships, making informed decisions, and achieving personal and professional success.
- **Growth Mindset:** Embrace the idea that your abilities can be developed through effort and learning. A growth mindset empowers you to view challenges as opportunities, persevere through difficulties, and continuously improve.
- **Self-Compassion:** Treat yourself with kindness and understanding when facing setbacks. Self-compassion allows you to navigate challenges with resilience and maintain motivation on your journey to personal growth.
- **Continuous Learning:** Commit to lifelong learning and curiosity. Exploring new ideas, seeking feedback, and expanding your knowledge will help you stay adaptable and open to new opportunities.
- **Practical Application:** Apply the strategies and exercises from this book in your daily life. Regular practice and reflection will help you integrate these concepts and see tangible results.

Moving Forward: Your Path to Success

The journey of self-discovery and personal growth is ongoing. As you move forward, carry the lessons learned from this book with you. Embrace the challenges and opportunities that come your way, and remember that growth is a continuous process.

Set new goals, seek out new experiences, and stay committed to your personal development. Whether you're striving for professional success, improved relationships, or personal fulfillment, the principles and practices outlined in this book will serve as valuable tools on your path.

Take the Next Step

Now that you've explored these concepts, take actionable steps towards applying them in your life:

1. **Set Personal Goals:** Identify specific areas where you want to grow and set clear, achievable goals. Create a plan of action and monitor your progress.
2. **Practice Self-Reflection:** Regularly reflect on your experiences, challenges, and achievements. Use self-reflection as a tool for continuous improvement.
3. **Engage with the Community:** Connect with others who share your interests and goals. Join groups, attend events, and engage in discussions to broaden your perspective and support your growth.
4. **Commit to Lifelong Learning:** Stay curious and open to new ideas. Continue to seek out resources, read books, and participate in learning opportunities to keep growing and evolving.

Embracing Your Potential

You have the power to shape your future and create a life of fulfillment and success. By embracing the principles of emotional intelligence, a growth mindset, and continuous learning, you are well-equipped to navigate the challenges and seize the opportunities that lie ahead.

Believe in your potential, trust in your journey, and remember that every step you take towards growth is a step towards a more meaningful and rewarding life. The path of self-discovery is uniquely yours, and each day presents a new opportunity to embrace change and pursue your passions.

Thank you for embarking on this journey with us. May you continue to grow, learn, and thrive in all aspects of your life.

12

Bonus Chapter: Letting Go Toolkit

The Power of Letting Go

In our journey through personal growth and emotional mastery, we've explored the importance of embracing change and overcoming challenges. As a complement to the core themes of this book, this bonus chapter presents the "Letting Go Toolkit"—a collection of practical tools and exercises designed to help you release what no longer serves you and embrace a more liberated and fulfilling life.

The ability to let go is a powerful practice that can lead to profound personal transformation. Whether you're letting go of old habits, negative thoughts, past hurts, or limiting beliefs, this toolkit provides actionable strategies to support your journey.

Tool 1: The Release Ritual

Purpose: To create a structured process for letting go of emotional burdens or limiting beliefs.

How It Works:

1. **Identify the Burden:** Write down what you want to let go of—this could be a past hurt, a negative belief, or a self-limiting habit.
2. **Create a Ritual:** Choose a symbolic act that represents letting go. This could be writing a letter and burning it, creating a visual representation and discarding it, or any other symbolic action that resonates with you.
3. **Perform the Ritual:** Engage in the ritual with intention, focusing on releasing the emotional attachment to what you've written or visualized.
4. **Reflect and Release:** After the ritual, take a moment to reflect on the experience. Notice any shifts in your feelings or mindset.

Example: Sarah struggled with the guilt of a past mistake. She wrote a letter detailing her feelings and burned it in a safe outdoor space. The act of burning the letter symbolized her release of the guilt and helped her move forward with a renewed sense of freedom.

Tool 2: The Forgiveness Exercise

Purpose: To facilitate forgiveness of others and yourself, freeing you from lingering resentment and self-blame.

How It Works:

1. **Identify the Source of Hurt:** Reflect on who or what you need to forgive. Write down the specific instances or

actions that have caused you pain.

2. **Write a Forgiveness Letter:** Draft a letter expressing your feelings and your decision to forgive. This letter is for you, so be honest and detailed.

3. **Release the Letter:** You can choose to keep, burn, or dispose of the letter as a symbolic act of forgiveness.

4. **Affirm Your Forgiveness:** Repeat affirmations of forgiveness and release. For example, "I choose to forgive and release this burden, allowing myself to move forward with peace."

Example: John held onto resentment towards a former business partner. By writing a forgiveness letter and performing a releasing ritual, he was able to let go of the lingering anger and focus on his new ventures with a clear mind.

Tool 3: The Gratitude Journal

Purpose: To shift your focus from what you're letting go of to what you're grateful for, fostering a positive mindset.

How It Works:

1. **Daily Entries:** Each day, write down three things you are grateful for. This can include big achievements or small everyday joys.

2. **Focus on the Positive:** Allow yourself to truly feel the gratitude as you write. Reflect on how these positive aspects of your life contribute to your well-being.

3. **Review Regularly:** Periodically review your entries to remind yourself of the positive changes and ongoing sources

of joy in your life.

Example: Emily started a gratitude journal to counterbalance her focus on past regrets. By consistently noting things she was grateful for, she developed a more positive outlook and found it easier to let go of negative thoughts.

Tool 4: The Mindful Letting Go Meditation

Purpose: To cultivate mindfulness and help you release stress and anxiety associated with letting go.

How It Works:

1. **Find a Quiet Space:** Sit in a comfortable position in a quiet place where you won't be disturbed.
2. **Focus on Your Breath:** Close your eyes and take deep, slow breaths. Allow yourself to relax and become present.
3. **Visualize Letting Go:** Picture a balloon carrying your burdens or worries. As you exhale, visualize the balloon floating away, taking with it your stress and concerns.
4. **Affirm Your Release:** Repeat a calming affirmation such as, "I release my worries and embrace peace." Continue to focus on your breath and visualization until you feel a sense of release.

Example: David used this meditation to manage his anxiety about a major life change. By visualizing his worries floating away, he found it easier to approach the change with calm and clarity.

Tool 5: The Boundary Setting Framework

Purpose: To help you establish and maintain healthy boundaries, which is crucial for letting go of relationships or situations that drain you.

How It Works:

1. **Identify Your Needs:** Reflect on areas where you need to set boundaries. This could be in relationships, work, or personal habits.
2. **Communicate Clearly:** Develop clear, assertive statements about your boundaries. For example, "I need time alone to recharge, so I'll be unavailable after 7 PM."
3. **Implement and Maintain:** Begin applying your boundaries consistently. Be prepared to assert them and reinforce them as needed.
4. **Reflect on the Impact:** Notice how setting these boundaries affects your well-being and relationships. Adjust as necessary to maintain balance.

Example: Lisa found herself overwhelmed by constant work demands. By setting clear boundaries around her work hours and communicating them to her colleagues, she regained control of her time and reduced her stress levels.

Tool 6: The Vision Board for Letting Go

Purpose: To create a visual representation of what you want to embrace and release, helping to clarify and focus your intentions.

How It Works:

1. **Gather Materials:** Collect magazines, printouts, or digital images that represent what you want to embrace and what you wish to release.
2. **Create Your Vision Board:** Arrange the images and words on a board or large paper. On one side, place images representing what you want to let go of; on the other side, place images representing your new goals and aspirations.
3. **Display and Reflect:** Place your vision board in a visible area where you can see it daily. Use it as a reminder of your intentions and goals.
4. **Update as Needed:** Regularly update your vision board to reflect changes in your goals and aspirations.

Example: Tom used a vision board to transition from a career he no longer enjoyed to a new path he was passionate about. The board helped him stay focused on his new direction and let go of his old career's constraints.

Embracing the Freedom of Letting Go

The tools and exercises in this Letting Go Toolkit are designed to support you in releasing what no longer serves you and embracing a more fulfilling and liberated life. By applying these practices, you can create space for new opportunities, growth, and joy.

Remember, letting go is not about forgetting but about freeing yourself from the past to make room for the future. As you integrate these tools into your life, trust in the process of transformation and celebrate the newfound freedom you create.

Thank you for exploring this bonus chapter. May these tools help you on your journey of self-discovery, growth, and empowerment.